DOVER·THRIFT·EDITIONS

Snake
and Other Poems

D. H. LAWRENCE

DOVER PUBLICATIONS, INC.
Mineola, New York

DOVER THRIFT EDITIONS

GENERAL EDITOR: PAUL NEGRI
EDITOR OF THIS VOLUME: BOB BLAISDELL

Bibliographical Note

This Dover edition, first published in 1999, is a new selection of D. H. Lawrence's poetry reprinted from standard texts.

Library of Congress Cataloging-in-Publication Data

Lawrence, D. H. (David Herbert), 1885–1930.
    Snake and other poems / D. H. Lawrence ; Bob Blaisdell, ed.
        p.   cm. — (Dover thrift editions)
    ISBN 0-486-40647-4 (pbk.)
    I. Blaisdell, Robert.   II. Title.   III. Series.
PR6023.A93A6   1999
821'.912—dc21   98–41016
                                                                          CIP

Manufactured in the United States of America
Dover Publications, Inc., 31 East 2nd Street, Mineola, N.Y. 11501

Note

David Herbert Lawrence was born in 1885 to a minister's daughter and a coal-miner in Eastwood, Nottinghamshire, in the north of England. He loved nature from boyhood and was an outstanding student, eventually earning a scholarship to attend college. He taught in an elementary school near London in 1909–1912 before health problems forced him to give up teaching. Through the modest success of his first three novels, including *Sons and Lovers*, and the appearance of poems and stories in Ford Maddox Hueffer's *The English Review*, Lawrence, with the encouragement of his wife-to-be, Frieda Weekley, set out to make his living as a writer.

In his writing over the next decade, he explored with unique clarity and subtlety some of the most sensitive aspects of married life, although he was often condemned for his candor. In 1915, *The Rainbow* was published but almost immediately suppressed by a nervous and self-righteous war-time England. *Women in Love*, though completed in 1916, was also shunned for its frankness about sexuality and individuality, and did not find a publisher until 1921. It was only at the end of his life that Lawrence was able to reach vast audiences. Before he died of tuberculosis in 1930, he had become famous, but unfortunately that fame came mostly from writing so-called "obscenity"—his last novel, *Lady Chatterley's Lover* (1928).

Lawrence authored some of the twentieth century's greatest short stories, novels, essays, criticism, travel writing, and poetry. So powerful is his fiction that it has overshadowed his poetry. A contemporary of Pound, Hardy, Eliot, and Yeats, his exuberance and intensity were unmatched by any of them. He wrote about love, marriage, family, class, art and culture in various genres and at various times again and again, much like a painter returning to the same landscape and attacking or appreciating it as the mood and moment touched him. His earlier poems are formally conventional, but consistent with the themes and insights of his later, freer work. His "animal" poems, including among others "Snake," "Bat," and the "Tortoise" series, are his most extraordinary verses—a strange and wonderful mixture of aggressive identification and awed appreciation of difference: they are explosively rhetorical and often humorous. These poems seem to owe much to Whitman, a writer Lawrence both admired and ridiculed (see his *Studies in Classic American Literature*).

In the late 1910s, when editors feared the uproar his fiction might cause for their magazines or publishing houses, several collections of poems—helped rather than hindered by his notoriety—came tumbling out. *Love Poems and Others* (1913), *Amores* (1916), *Look! We Have Come Through!* (1917), and *Tortoises* (1921) are represented in this selection, with an ample selection coming from poems published in periodicals in 1921 and 1922 before their appearance in *Birds, Beasts and Flowers* (1923). Because of copyright restrictions, the sharp, bitter, often epigrammatic poems collected in *Pansies* (1929) and *Nettles* (1930) are not included in this edition.

Contents

From *Tortoises* (1921)

From Periodicals

Bei Hennef

The little river twittering in the twilight,
The wan, wondering look of the pale sky,
    This is almost bliss.

And everything shut up and gone to sleep,
All the troubles and anxieties and pain
    Gone under the twilight.

Only the twilight now, and the soft "Sh!" of the river
    That will last for ever.

And at last I know my love for you is here,
I can see it all, it is whole like the twilight,
It is large, so large, I could not see it before
Because of the little lights and flickers and interruptions,
    Troubles, anxieties and pains.

    You are the call and I am the answer,
    You are the wish, and I the fulfilment,
    You are the night, and I the day.
        What else—it is perfect enough,
        It is perfectly complete,
        You and I,
        What more——?
Strange, how we suffer in spite of this!

A Collier's Wife

Somebody's knocking at the door
    Mother, come down and see.
—I's think it's nobbut a beggar,
    Say, I'm busy.

It's not a beggar, mother,—hark
    How hard he knocks . . .
—Eh, tha'rt a mard-'arsed kid,
    'E'll gi'e thee socks!

Shout an' ax what 'e wants,
    I canna come down.
—'E says "Is it Arthur Holliday's?"
    Say "Yes," tha clown.

'E says, "Tell your mother as 'er mester's
    Got hurt i' th' pit."
What—oh my sirs, 'e never says that,
    That's niver it.

Come out o' the way an' let me see,
    Eh, there's no peace!
An' stop thy scraightin', childt,
    Do shut thy face.

"Your mester's 'ad an accident,
    An' they're ta'ein 'im i' th' ambulance
To Nottingham,"—Eh dear o' me
    If 'e's not a man for mischance!

Wheers he hurt this time, lad?
    —I dunna know,
They on'y towd me it wor bad—
    It would be so!

Eh, what a man!—an' that cobbly road,
    They'll jolt him a'most to death,
I'm sure he's in for some trouble
    Nigh every time he takes breath.

Out o' my way, childt—dear o' me, wheer
    Have I put his clean stockings and shirt;
Goodness knows if they'll be able
    To take off his pit dirt.

An' what a moan he'll make—there niver
    Was such a man for a fuss
If anything ailed him—at any rate
    I shan't have him to nuss.

I do hope it's not very bad!
    Eh, what a shame it seems
As some should ha'e hardly a smite o' trouble
    An' others has reams.

It's a shame as 'e should be knocked about
    Like this, I'm sure it is!
He's had twenty accidents, if he's had one;
    Owt bad, an' it's his.

There's one thing, we 'll have peace for a bit,
    Thank Heaven for a peaceful house;
An' there's compensation, sin' it's accident,
    An' club money—I nedn't grouse.

An' a fork an' a spoon he'll want, an' what else;
    I s'll never catch that train—
What a trapse it is if a man gets hurt—
    I s'd think he'll get right again.

The Schoolmaster

I

A SNOWY DAY IN SCHOOL

All the slow school hours, round the irregular hum of the class,
Have pressed immeasurable spaces of hoarse silence
Muffling my mind, as snow muffles the sounds that pass
Down the soiled street. We have pattered the lessons ceaselessly—

But the faces of the boys, in the brooding, yellow light
Have shone for me like a crowded constellation of stars,

Like full-blown flowers dimly shaking at the night,
Like floating froth on an ebbing shore in the moon.

Out of each star, dark, strange beams that disquiet:
In the open depths of each flower, dark restless drops:
Twin bubbles, shadow-full of mystery and challenge in the foam's
     whispering riot:
—How can I answer the challenge of so many eyes?—A voice

The thick snow is crumpled on the roof, it plunges down
Awfully. Must I call back those hundred eyes—A voice
Wakes from the hum, faltering about a noun—
My question! My God, I must break from this hoarse silence

That rustles beyond the stars to me.—There,
I have startled a hundred eyes, and I must look
Them an answer back. It is more than I can bear.

The snow descends as if the dull sky shook
In flakes of shadow down; and through the gap
Between the ruddy schools sweeps one black rook.

The rough snowball in the playground stands huge and still
With fair flakes settling down on it.—Beyond, the town
Is lost in the shadowed silence the skies distil.

And all things are possessed by silence, and they can brood
Wrapped up in the sky's dim space of hoarse silence
Earnestly—and oh for me this class is a bitter rood.

II
THE BEST OF SCHOOL

     The blinds are drawn because of the sun,
     And the boys and the room in a colourless gloom
     Of under-water float: bright ripples run
     Across the walls as the blinds are blown
     To let the sunlight in; and I,
     As I sit on the beach of the class alone,
     Watch the boys in their summer blouses,
     As they write, their round heads busily bowed:

And one after another rouses
And lifts his face and looks at me,
And my eyes meet his very quietly,
Then he turns again to his work, with glee.

With glee he turns, with a little glad
Ecstasy of work he turns from me,
An ecstasy surely sweet to be had.

And very sweet while the sunlight waves
In the fresh of the morning, it is to be
A teacher of these young boys, my slaves
Only as swallows are slaves to the eaves
They build upon, as mice are slaves
To the man who threshes and sows the sheaves.

              Oh, sweet it is
To feel the lads' looks light on me,
Then back in a swift, bright flutter to work,
As birds who are stealing turn and flee.

Touch after touch I feel on me
As their eyes glance at me for the grain
Of rigour they taste delightedly.

                And all the class,
As tendrils reached out yearningly
Slowly rotate till they touch the tree
That they cleave unto, that they leap along
Up to their lives—so they to me.

So do they cleave and cling to me,
So I lead them up, so do they twine
Me up, caress and clothe with free
Fine foliage of lives this life of mine;
The lowest stem of this life of mine,
The old hard stem of my life
That bears aloft towards rarer skies
My top of life, that buds on high
Amid the high wind's enterprise.

They all do clothe my ungrowing life
With a rich, a thrilled young clasp of life;
A clutch of attachment, like parenthood,
Mounts up to my heart, and I find it good.

And I lift my head upon the troubled tangled world, and though
   the pain
Of living my life were doubled, I still have this to comfort
   and sustain,
I have such swarming sense of lives at the base of me, such
   sense of lives,
Clustering upon me, reaching up, as each after the other strives
To follow my life aloft to the fine wild air of life and the storm
   of thought,
And though I scarcely see the boys, or know that they are there,
   distraught
As I am with living my life in earnestness, still progressively and
   alone,
Though they cling, forgotten the most part, not companions,
   scarcely known
To me—yet still because of the sense of their closeness clinging
   densely to me,
And slowly fingering up my stem and following all tinily
The way that I have gone and now am leading, they are dear to me.

They keep me assured, and when my soul feels lonely,
All mistrustful of thrusting its shoots where only
I alone am living, then it keeps
Me comforted to feel the warmth that creeps
Up dimly from their striving; it heartens my strife:
And when my heart is chill with loneliness,
Then comforts it the creeping tenderness
Of all the strays of life that climb my life.

III
AFTERNOON IN SCHOOL
THE LAST LESSON

When will the bell ring, and end this weariness?
How long have they tugged the leash, and strained apart
My pack of unruly hounds: I cannot start
Them again on a quarry of knowledge they hate to hunt,

I can haul them and urge them no more.
No more can I endure to bear the brunt
Of the books that lie out on the desks: a full three score
Of several insults of blotted pages and scrawl
Of slovenly work that they have offered me.
I am sick, and tired more than any thrall
Upon the woodstacks working weariedly.

                        And shall I take
The last dear fuel and heap it on my soul
Till I rouse my will like a fire to consume
Their dross of indifference, and burn the scroll
Of their insults in punishment?—I will not!
I will not waste myself to embers for them,
Not all for them shall the fires of my life be hot.
For myself a heap of ashes of weariness, till sleep
Shall have raked the embers clear: I will keep
Some of my strength for myself, for if I should sell
It all for them, I should hate them—
        —I will sit and wait for the bell.

Cruelty and Love*

What large, dark hands are those at the window
Grasping in the golden light
Which weaves its way through the evening wind
    At my heart's delight?

Ah, only the leaves! But in the west
I see a redness suddenly come
Into the evening's anxious breast—
    'Tis the wound of love goes home!

The woodbine creeps abroad
Calling low to her lover:
    The sunlight flirt who all the day
    Has poised above her lips in play
    And stolen kisses, shallow and gay

---

*First published in 1913 in *Love Poems and Others,* and retitled "Love on the Farm"
  when it appeared in *Collected Poems* (1928).

Of pollen, now has gone away—
She woos the moth with her sweet, low word;
And when above her his moth-wings hover
Then her bright breast she will uncover
And yield her honey-drop to her lover.

Into the yellow, evening glow
Saunters a man from the farm below;
Leans, and looks in at the low-built shed
Where the swallow has hung her marriage bed.
    The bird lies warm against the wall.
    She glances quick her startled eyes
    Towards him, then she turns away
    Her small head, making warm display
    Of red upon the throat. Her terrors sway
    Her out of the nest's warm, busy ball,
    Whose plaintive cry is heard as she flies
    In one blue stoop from out the sties
    Into the twilight's empty hall.
Oh, water-hen, beside the rushes
Hide your quaintly scarlet blushes,
Still your quick tail, lie still as dead,
Till the distance folds over his ominous tread!

The rabbit presses back her ears,
Turns back her liquid, anguished eyes
And crouches low; then with wild spring
Spurts from the terror of *his* oncoming;
To be choked back, the wire ring
Her frantic effort throttling:
    Piteous brown ball of quivering fears!
Ah, soon in his large, hard hands she dies,
And swings all loose from the swing of his walk!
Yet calm and kindly are his eyes
And ready to open in brown surprise
Should I not answer to his talk
Or should he my tears surmise.

I hear his hand on the latch, and rise from my chair
Watching the door open; he flashes bare
His strong teeth in a smile, and flashes his eyes
In a smile like triumph upon me; then careless-wise

He flings the rabbit soft on the table board
And comes towards me: ah! the uplifted sword
Of his hand against my bosom! and oh, the broad
Blade of his glance that asks me to applaud
His coming! With his hand he turns my face to him
And caresses me with his fingers that still smell grim
Of the rabbit's fur! God, I am caught in a snare!
I know not what fine wire is round my throat;
I only know I let him finger there
My pulse of life, and let him nose like a stoat
Who sniffs with joy before he drinks the blood.

And down his mouth comes to my mouth! and down
His bright dark eyes come over me, like a hood
Upon my mind! his lips meet mine, and a flood
Of sweet fire sweeps across me, so I drown
Against him, die, and find death good.

A Baby Running Barefoot

When the bare feet of the baby beat across the grass
The little white feet nod like white flowers in the wind,
They poise and run like ripples lapping across the water;
And the sight of their white play among the grass
Is like a little robin's song, winsome,
Or as two white butterflies settle in the cup of one flower
For a moment, then away with a flutter of wings.

I long for the baby to wander hither to me
Like a wind-shadow wandering over the water,
So that she can stand on my knee
With her little bare feet in my hands,
Cool like syringa buds,
Firm and silken like pink young peony flowers.

A Baby Asleep After Pain

As a drenched, drowned bee
Hangs numb and heavy from a bending flower,
So clings to me
My baby, her brown hair brushed with wet tears
And laid against her cheek;

Her soft white legs hanging heavily over my arm
Swinging heavily to my movement as I walk.
    My sleeping baby hangs upon my life,
Like a burden she hangs on me.
    She has always seemed so light,
But now she is wet with tears and numb with pain
Even her floating hair sinks heavily,
    Reaching downwards;
As the wings of a drenched, drowned bee
    Are a heaviness, and a weariness.

Monologue of a Mother

This is the last of all, this is the last!
I must hold my hands, and turn my face to the fire,
I must watch my dead days fusing together in the dross,
Shape after shape, and scene after scene from my past
Fusing to one dead mass in the sinking fire
Where the ash on the dying coals grows swiftly, like heavy moss.

Strange he is, my son, whom I have awaited like a lover,
Strange to me like a captive in a foreign country, haunting
The confines and gazing out on the land where the wind is free;
White and gaunt, with wistful eyes that hover
Always on the distance, as if his soul were chaunting
The monotonous weird of departure away from me.

Like a strange white bird blown out of the frozen seas,
Like a bird from the far north blown with a broken wing
Into our sooty garden, he drags and beats
From place to place perpetually, seeking release
From me, from the hand of my love which creeps up, needing
His happiness, whilst he in displeasure retreats.

I must look away from him, for my faded eyes
Like a cringing dog at his heels offend him now,
Like a toothless hound pursuing him with my will,
Till he chafes at my crouching persistence, and a sharp spark flies
In my soul from under the sudden frown of his brow,
As he blenches and turns away, and my heart stands still.

This is the last, it will not be any more.
All my life I have borne the burden of myself,
All the long years of sitting in my husband's house,
Never have I said to myself as he closed the door:
"Now I am caught!—You are hopelessly lost, O Self,
You are frightened with joy, my heart, like a frightened mouse."

Three times have I offered myself, three times rejected.
It will not be any more. No more, my son, my son!
Never to know the glad freedom of obedience, since long ago
The angel of childhood kissed me and went. I expected
Another would take me,—and now, my son, O my son,
I must sit awhile and wait, and never know
The loss of myself, till death comes, who cannot fail.

Death, in whose service is nothing of gladness, takes me;
For the lips and the eyes of God are behind a veil.
And the thought of the lipless voice of the Father shakes me
With fear, and fills my eyes with the tears of desire,
And my heart rebels with anguish as night draws nigher.

The Wild Common

The quick sparks on the gorse bushes are leaping,
Little jets of sunlight-texture imitating flame;
Above them, exultant, the pee-wits are sweeping:
They are lords of the desolate wastes of sadness their screamings
    proclaim.

Rabbits, handfuls of brown earth, lie
Low-rounded on the mournful grass they have bitten down to the quick.
Are they asleep?—Are they alive?—Now see, when I
Move my arms the hill bursts and heaves under their spurting kick.

The common flaunts bravely; but below, from the rushes
Crowds of glittering king-cups surge to challenge the blossoming
    bushes;
There the lazy streamlet pushes
Its curious course mildly; here it wakes again, leaps, laughs and
    gushes.

Into a deep pond, an old sheep-dip,
Dark, overgrown with willows, cool, with the brook ebbing through
    so slow,
Naked on the steep, soft lip
Of the bank I stand watching my own white shadow quivering
    to and fro.

What if the gorse flowers shrivelled and kissing were lost?
Without the pulsing waters, where were the marigolds and the songs
    of the brook?
If my veins and my breasts with love embossed
Withered, my insolent soul would be gone like flowers that the
    hot wind took.

So my soul like a passionate woman turns,
Filled with remorseful terror to the man she scorned, and her love
For myself in my own eyes' laughter burns,
Runs ecstatic over the pliant folds rippling down to my belly
    from the breast-lights above.

Over my sunlit skin the warm, clinging air,
Rich with the songs of seven larks singing at once, goes kissing me glad.
And the soul of the wind and my blood compare
Their wandering happiness, and the wind, wasted in liberty, drifts on
    and is sad.

Oh but the water loves me and folds me,
Plays with me, sways me, lifts me and sinks me as though it were
    living blood,
Blood of a heaving woman who holds me,
Owning my supple body a rare glad thing, supremely good.

"And Oh—
That the Man I Am
Might Cease to Be—"

No, now I wish the sunshine would stop,
and the white shining houses, and the gay red flowers on the balconies
and the bluish mountains beyond, would be crushed out
between two valves of darkness;
the darkness falling, the darkness rising, with muffled sound
obliterating everything.

I wish that whatever props up the walls of light
would fall, and darkness would come hurling heavily down,
and it would be thick black dark for ever.
Not sleep, which is grey with dreams,
nor death, which quivers with birth,
but heavy, sealing darkness, silence, all immovable.

What is sleep?
It goes over me, like a shadow over a hill,
but it does not alter me, nor help me.
And death would ache still, I am sure;
it would be lambent, uneasy.
I wish it would be completely dark everywhere,
inside me, and out, heavily dark
utterly.

She Looks Back

The pale bubbles
The lovely pale-gold bubbles of the globe-flowers
In a great swarm clotted and single
Went rolling in the dusk towards the river
To where the sunset hung its wan gold cloths;
And you stood alone, watching them go,
And that mother-love like a demon drew you from me
Towards England.

Along the road, after nightfall,
Along the glamorous birch-tree avenue
Across the river levels
We went in silence, and you staring to England.

So then there shone within the jungle darkness
Of the long, lush under-grass, a glow-worm's sudden
Green lantern of pure light, a little, intense, fusing triumph,
White and haloed with fire-mist, down in the tangled darkness.

Then you put your hand in mine again, kissed me,
    and we struggled to be together.
And the little electric flashes went with us, in the grass,
Tiny lighthouses, little souls of lanterns, courage
    burst into an explosion of green light
Everywhere down in the grass, where darkness was
    ravelled in darkness.

Still, the kiss was a touch of bitterness on my mouth
Like salt, burning in.
And my hand withered in your hand.
For you were straining with a wild heart, back, back again,
Back to those children you had left behind, to all
  the æons of the past.
And I was here in the under-dusk of the Isar.

At home, we leaned in the bedroom window
Of the old Bavarian Gasthaus,
And the frogs in the pool beyond thrilled with exuberance,
Like a boiling pot the pond crackled with happiness,
Like a rattle a child spins round for joy, the night rattled
With the extravagance of the frogs,
And you leaned your cheek on mine,
And I suffered it, wanting to sympathise.

At last, as you stood, your white gown falling from your breasts,
You looked into my eyes, and said: "But this is joy!"
I acquiesced again.
But the shadow of lying was in your eyes,
The mother in you, fierce as a murderess, glaring to England,
Yearning towards England, towards your young children, .
Insisting upon your motherhood, devastating.

Still, the joy was there also, you spoke truly,
The joy was not to be driven off so easily;
Stronger than fear or destructive mother-love, it stood flickering;
The frogs helped also, whirring away.
Yet how I have learned to know that look in your eyes
Of horrid sorrow!
How I know that glitter of salt,—dry, sterile, sharp, corrosive salt!
Not tears, but white sharp brine
Making hideous your eyes.

I have seen it, felt it in my mouth, my throat, my chest, my belly,
Burning of powerful salt, burning, eating through my defenceless
  nakedness,
I have been thrust into white, sharp crystals,
Writhing, twisting, superpenetrated.

Ah, Lot's Wife, Lot's Wife!
The pillar of salt, the whirling, horrible column of salt, like a waterspout
That has enveloped me!
Snow of salt, white, burning, eating salt
In which I have writhed.

Lot's Wife! — Not Wife, but Mother.
I have learned to curse your motherhood,
You pillar of salt accursed.
I have cursed motherhood because of you,
Accursed, base motherhood!

I long for the time to come, when the curse against you will have
    gone out of my heart.
But it has not gone yet.
Nevertheless, once, the frogs, the globe-flowers of Bavaria,
    the glow-worms
Gave me sweet lymph against the salt-burns,
There is a kindness in the very rain.

Therefore, even in the hour of my deepest, passionate malediction
I try to remember it is also well between us.
That you are with me in the end.
That you never look quite back; nine-tenths, ah, more
You look round over your shoulder;
But never quite back.

Nevertheless the curse against you is still in my heart
Like a deep, deep burn.
The curse against all mothers.
All mothers who fortify themselves in motherhood, devastating
    the vision.
They are accursed, and the curse is not taken off
It burns within me like a deep, old burn,
And oh, I wish it was better.

Frohnleichnam

You have come your way, I have come my way;
You have stepped across your people, carelessly, hurting them all;
I have stepped across my people, and hurt them in spite of my care.

But steadily, surely, and notwithstanding
We have come our ways and met at last
Here in this upper room.

Here the balcony
Overhangs the street where the bullock-wagons slowly
Go by with their loads of green and silver birch trees
For the feast of Corpus Christi.

Here from the balcony
We look over the growing wheat, where the jade-green river
Goes between the pine-woods,
Over and beyond to where the many mountains
Stand in their blueness, flashing with snow and the morning.

I have done; a quiver of exultation goes through me, like the first
Breeze of the morning through a narrow white birch.
You glow at last like the mountain tops when they catch
Day and make magic in heaven.

At last I can throw away world without end, and meet you
Unsheathed and naked and narrow and white;
At last you can throw immortality off, and I see you
Glistening with all the moment and all your beauty.

Shameless and callous I love you;
Out of indifference I love you;
Out of mockery we dance together,
Out of the sunshine into the shadow,
Passing across the shadow into the sunlight,
Out of sunlight to shadow.

As we dance
Your eyes take all of me in as a communication;
As we dance
I see you, ah, in full!
Only to dance together in triumph of being together
Two white ones, sharp, vindicated,
Shining and touching,
Is heaven of our own, sheer with repudiation.

In the Dark

A blotch of pallor stirs beneath the high
Square picture-dusk, the window of dark sky.

A sound subdued in the darkness: tears!
As if a bird in difficulty up the valley steers.

"Why have you gone to the window? Why don't you sleep?
How you have wakened me!—But why, why do you weep?"

"*I am afraid of you, I am afraid, afraid!
There is something in you destroys me——!*"

"You have dreamed and are not awake, come here to me."
"*No, I have wakened. It is you, you are cruel to me!*"

"My dear!"—"*Yes, yes, you are cruel to me. You cast
A shadow over my breasts that will kill me at last.*"

"Come!"—"*No, I'm a thing of life. I give
You armfuls of sunshine, and you won't let me live.*"

"Nay, I'm too sleepy!"—"*Ah, you are horrible;
You stand before me like ghosts, like a darkness upright.*"

"I!"—"*How can you treat me so, and love me?
My feet have no hold, you take the sky from above me.*"

"My dear, the night is soft and eternal, no doubt
You love it!"—"*It is dark, it kills me, I am put out.*"

"My dear, when you cross the street in the sunshine, surely
Your own small night goes with you. Why treat it so poorly?"

"*No, no, I dance in the sun, I'm a thing of life—*"
"Even then it is dark behind you. Turn round, my wife."

"*No, how cruel you are, you people the sunshine
With shadows!*"—"With yours I people the sunshine,
    yours and mine——"

"In the darkness we all are gone, we are gone
  with the trees
And the restless river;—we are lost and gone
  with all these."

"But I am myself, I have nothing to do with these."
"Come back to bed, let us sleep on our mysteries.

"Come to me here, and lay your body by mine,
And I will be all the shadow, you the shine.

"Come, you are cold, the night has frightened you.
Hark at the river! It pants as it hurries through

"The pine-woods. How I love them so, in their
  mystery of not-to-be."
"—But let me be myself, not a river or a tree."

"Kiss me! How cold you are!—Your little breasts
Are bubbles of ice. Kiss me!—You know how it rests

"One to be quenched, to be given up, to be gone
  in the dark;
To be blown out, to let night dowse the spark.

"But never mind, my love. Nothing matters,
  save sleep;
Save you, and me, and sleep; all the rest will keep."

Gloire de Dijon

When she rises in the morning
I linger to watch her;
She spreads the bath-cloth underneath the window
And the sunbeams catch her
Glistening white on the shoulders,
While down her sides the mellow
Golden shadow glows as
She stoops to the sponge, and her swung breasts
Sway like full-blown yellow
Gloire de Dijon roses.

She drips herself with water, and her shoulders
Glisten as silver, they crumple up
Like wet and falling roses, and I listen
For the sluicing of their rain-dishevelled petals.
In the window full of sunlight
Concentrates her golden shadow
Fold on fold, until it glows as
Mellow as the glory roses.

A Youth Mowing

There are four men mowing down by the Isar;
I can hear the swish of the scythe-strokes, four
Sharp breaths taken: yea, and I
Am sorry for what's in store.

The first man out of the four that's mowing
Is mine, I claim him once and for all;
Though it's sorry I am, on his young feet, knowing
None of the trouble he's led to stall.

As he sees me bringing the dinner, he lifts
His head as proud as a deer that looks
Shoulder-deep out of the corn; and wipes
His scythe-blade bright, unhooks

The scythe-stone and over the stubble to me.
Lad, thou hast gotten a child in me,
Laddie, a man thou'lt ha'e to be,
Yea, though I'm sorry for thee.

Quite Forsaken

What pain, to wake and miss you!
    To wake with a tightened heart,
And mouth reaching forward to kiss you!

This then at last is the dawn, and the bell
    Clanging at the farm! Such bewilderment
Comes with the sight of the room, I cannot tell.

It is raining. Down the half-obscure road
    Four labourers pass with their scythes
Dejectedly;—a huntsman goes by with his load:

A gun, and a bunched-up deer, its four little feet
    Clustered dead.—And this is the dawn
For which I wanted the night to retreat!

Fireflies in the Corn

She speaks.
Look at the little darlings in the corn!
    The rye is taller than you, who think yourself
So high and mighty: look how the heads are borne
    Dark and proud on the sky, like a number of knights
Passing with spears and pennants and manly scorn.

Knights indeed!—much knight I know will ride
    With his head held high-serene against the sky!
Limping and following rather at my side
    Moaning for me to love him!—Oh darling rye
How I adore you for your simple pride!

And the dear, dear fireflies wafting in between
    And over the swaying corn-stalks, just above
All the dark-feathered helmets, like little green
    Stars come low and wandering here for love
Of these dark knights, shedding their delicate sheen!

I thank you I do, you happy creatures, you dears
    Riding the air, and carrying all the time
Your little lanterns behind you! Ah, it cheers
    My soul to see you settling and trying to climb
The corn-stalks, tipping with fire the spears.

All over the dim corn's motion, against the blue
    Dark sky of night, a wandering glitter, a swarm
Of questing brilliant souls going out with their true
    Proud knights to battle! Sweet, how I warm
My poor, my perished soul with the sight of you!

A Doe at Evening

As I went through the marshes
a doe sprang out of the corn
and flashed up the hill-side
leaving her fawn.

On the sky-line
she moved round to watch,
she pricked a fine black blotch
on the sky.

I looked at her
and felt her watching;
I because a strange being.
Still, I had my right to be there with her.

Her nimble shadow trotting
along the sky-line, she
put back her fine, level-balanced head.
And I knew her.

Ah yes, being male, is not my head hard-balanced, antlered?
Are not my haunches light?
Has she not fled on the same wind with me?
Does not my fear cover her fear?

Both Sides of the Medal

And because you love me
think you you do not hate me?
Ha, since you love me
to ecstasy
it follows you hate me to ecstasy.

Because when you hear me
go down the road outside the house
you must come to the window to watch me go,
do you think it is pure worship?

Because, when I sit in the room,
here, in my own house,
and you want to enlarge yourself with this friend of mine,
such a friend as he is,
yet you cannot get beyond your awareness of me
you are held back by my being in the same world with you,
do you think it is bliss alone?
sheer harmony?

No doubt if I were dead, you must
reach into death after me,
but would not your hate reach even more madly than your love?
your impassioned, unfinished hate?

Since you have a passion for me,
as I for you,
does not that passion stand in your way like a Balaam's ass?
and am I not Balaam's ass
golden-mouthed occasionally?
But mostly, do you not detest my bray?

Since you are confined in the orbit of me
do you not loathe the confinement?
Is not even the beauty and peace of an orbit
an intolerable prison to you,
as it is to everybody?

But we will learn to submit
each of us to the balanced, eternal orbit
wherein we circle on our fate
in strange conjunction.

What is chaos, my love?
It is not freedom.
A disarray of falling stars coming to nought.

Spring Morning

Ah, through the open door
Is there an almond tree
Aflame with blossom!
—Let us fight no more.

Among the pink and blue
Of the sky and the almond flowers
A sparrow flutters,
        —We have come through,

It is really spring!—See,
When he thinks himself alone
How he bullies the flowers.
        —Ah, you and me

How happy we'll be!—See him
He clouts the tufts of flowers
In his impudence.
        —But, did you dream

It would be so bitter? Never mind
It is finished, the spring is here.
And we're going to be summer-happy
        And summer-kind.

We have died, we have slain and been slain,
We are not our old selves any more.
I feel new and eager
        To start again.

It is gorgeous to live and forget.
And to feel quite new.
See the bird in the flowers?—he's making
        A rare to-do!

He thinks the whole blue sky
Is much less than the bit of blue egg
He's got in his nest—we'll be happy
        You and I, I and you.

With nothing to fight any more—
In each other, at least.
See, how gorgeous the world is
        Outside the door!

Wedlock

I

Come, my little one, closer up against me,
Creep right up, with your round head pushed in my breast.

How I love all of you! Do you feel me wrap you
Up with myself and my warmth, like a flame round the wick?

And how I am not at all, except a flame that mounts off you.
Where I touch you, I flame into being;—but is it me, or you?

That round head pushed in my chest, like a nut in its socket,
And I the swift bracts that sheathe it: those breasts, those
   thighs and knees,

Those shoulders so warm and smooth: I feel that I
Am a sunlight upon them, that shines them into being.

But how lovely to be you! Creep closer in, that I am more.
I spread over you! How lovely, your round head, your arms,

Your breasts, your knees and feet! I feel that we
Are a bonfire of oneness, me flame flung leaping round you,
You the core of the fire, crept into me.

II

And oh, my little one, you whom I enfold,
How quaveringly I depend on you, to keep me alive.
Like a flame on a wick!

I, the man who enfolds you and holds you close,
How my soul cleaves to your bosom as I clasp you,
The very quick of my being!

Suppose you didn't want me! I should sink down
Like a light that has no sustenance
And sinks low.

Cherish me, my tiny one, cherish me who enfold you.
Nourish me, and endue me, I am only of you,
I am your issue.

How full and big like a robust, happy flame
When I enfold you, and you creep into me,
And my life is fierce at its quick
Where it comes off you!

III

My little one, my big one,
My bird, my brown sparrow in my breast.
My squirrel clutching in to me;
My pigeon, my little one, so warm
So close, breathing so still.

My little one, my big one,
I, who am so fierce and strong, enfolding you,
If you start away from my breast, and leave me,
How suddenly I shall go down into nothing
Like a flame that falls of a sudden.

And you will be before me, tall and towering,
And I shall be wavering uncertain
Like a sunken flame that grasps for support.

IV

But now I am full and strong and certain
With you there firm at the core of me
Keeping me.

How sure I feel, how warm and strong and happy
For the future! How sure the future is within me;
I am like a seed with a perfect flower enclosed.

I wonder what it will be,
What will come forth of us.
What flower, my love?

No matter, I am so happy,
I feel like a firm, rich, healthy root,
Rejoicing in what is to come.

How I depend on you utterly
My little one, my big one!
How everything that will be, will not be of me,
Nor of either of us,
But of both of us.

V

And think, there will something come forth from us.
We two, folded so small together,
There will something come forth from us.
Children, acts, utterance
Perhaps only happiness.

Perhaps only happiness will come forth from us.
Old sorrow, and new happiness.
Only that one newness.

But that is all I want.
And I am sure of that.
We are sure of that.

VI

And yet all the while you are you, you are not me.
And I am I, I am never you.
How awfully distinct and far off from each other's
    being we are!

Yet I am glad.
I am so glad there is always you beyond my scope,
Something that stands over,
Something I shall never be,
That I shall always wonder over, and wait for,
Look for like the breath of life as long as I live,
Still waiting for you, however old you are, and I am,
I shall always wonder over you, and look for you.

And you will always be with me.
I shall never cease to be filled with newness,
Having you near me.

"She Said as Well to Me"

She said as well to me: "Why are you ashamed?
That little bit of your chest that shows between
the gap of your shirt, why cover it up?
Why shouldn't your legs and your good strong thighs
be rough and hairy?—I'm glad they are like that.
You are shy, you silly, you silly shy thing.

Men are the shyest creatures, they never will come
out of their covers. Like any snake
slipping into its bed of dead leaves, you hurry into your clothes.
And I love you so! Straight and clean and all of a piece is the
    body of a man,
such an instrument, a spade, like a spear, or an oar,
such a joy to me—"
So she laid her hands and pressed them down my sides,
so that I began to wonder over myself, and what I was.

She said to me: "What an instrument, your body!
single and perfectly distinct from everything else!
What a tool in the hands of the Lord!
Only God could have brought it to its shape.
It feels as if his handgrasp, wearing you
had polished you and hollowed you,
hollowed this groove in your sides, grasped you under the breasts
and brought you to the very quick of your form,
subtler than an old, soft-worn fiddle-bow.

"When I was a child, I loved my father's riding-whip
that he used so often.
I loved to handle it, it seemed like a near part of him.
So I did his pens, and the jasper seal on his desk.
Something seemed to surge through me when I touched them.

"So it is with you, but here
The joy I feel!
God knows what I feel, but it is joy!
Look, you are clean and fine and singled out!
I admire you so, you are beautiful: this clean sweep of your sides,
    this firmness, this hard mould!
I would die rather than have it injured with one scar.
I wish I could grip you like the fist of the Lord,
and have you—"

So she said, and I wondered,
feeling trammelled and hurt.
It did not make me free.

Now I say to her: "No tool, no instrument, no God!
Don't touch me and appreciate me.
It is an infamy.

You would think twice before you touched a weasel on a fence
as it lifts its straight white throat.
Your hand would not be so flig and easy.
Nor the adder we saw asleep with her head on her shoulder,
curled up in the sunshine like a princess;
when she lifted her head in delicate, startled wonder
you did not stretch forward to caress her
though she looked rarely beautiful
and a miracle as she glided delicately away, with such dignity.
And the young bull in the field, with his wrinkled, sad face,
you are afraid if he rises to his feet,
though he is all wistful and pathetic, like a monolith, arrested, static.

"Is there nothing in me to make you hesitate?
I tell you there is all these.
And why should you overlook them in me?—"

New Heaven and Earth

I

And so I cross into another world
shyly and in homage linger for an invitation
from this unknown that I would trespass on.

I am very glad, and all alone in the world,
all alone, and very glad, in a new world
where I am disembarked at last.

I could cry with joy, because I am in the new world, just ventured in.
I could cry with joy, and quite freely, there is nobody to know.

And whosoever the unknown people of this unknown world may be
they will never understand my weeping for joy to be adventuring
    among them
because it will still be a gesture of the old world I am making
which they will not understand, because it is quite, quite foreign
    to them.

II

I was so weary of the world
I was so sick of it
everything was tainted with myself,

skies, trees, flowers, birds, water,
people, houses, streets, vehicles, machines,
nations, armies, war, peace-talking,
work, recreation, governing, anarchy,
It was all tainted with myself, I knew it all to start with
because it was all myself.

When I gathered flowers, I knew it was myself plucking my own
     flowering.
When I went in a train, I knew it was myself travelling by my own
     invention.
When I heard the cannon of the war, I listened with my own ears
     to my own destruction.
When I saw the torn dead, I knew it was my own torn dead body.
It was all me, I had done it all in my own flesh.

III
I shall never forget the maniacal horror of it all in the end
when everything was me, I knew it all already, I anticipated it all
     in my soul
because I was the author and the result
I was the God and the creation at once;
creator, I looked at my creation;
created, I looked at myself, the creator:
it was a maniacal horror in the end.

I was a lover, I kissed the woman I loved,
and God of horror, I was kissing also myself.
I was a father and a begetter of children,
and oh, oh horror, I was begetting and conceiving in my own body.

IV
At last came death, sufficiency of death,
and that at last relieved me, I died.
I buried my beloved; it was good, I buried myself and was gone.
War came, and every hand raised to murder;
very good, very good, every hand raised to murder!
Very good, very good, I am a murderer!
It is good, I can murder and murder, and see them fall
the mutilated, horror-struck youths, a multitude
one on another, and then in clusters together
smashed, all oozing with blood, and burned in heaps
going up in a fœtid smoke to get rid of them

the murdered bodies of youths and men in heaps
and heaps and heaps and horrible reeking heaps
till it is almost enough, till I am reduced perhaps;
thousands and thousands of gaping, hideous foul dead
that are youths and men and me
being burned with oil, and consumed in corrupt thick smoke, that rolls
and taints and blackens the sky, till at last it is dark, dark as night,
   or death, or hell
and I am dead, and trodden to nought in the smoke-sodden tomb;
dead and trodden to nought in the sour black earth
of the tomb; dead and trodden to nought, trodden to nought.

Baby Tortoise

You know what it is to be born alone,
Baby tortoise!

The first day to heave your feet little by little from the shell,
Not yet awake,
And remain lapsed on earth,
Not quite alive.

A tiny, fragile, half-animate bean.

To open your tiny beak-mouth, that looks as if it would never open,
Like some iron door;
To lift the upper hawk-beak from the lower base
And reach your skinny little neck
And take your first bite at some dim bit of herbage,
Alone, small insect,
Tiny bright-eye,
Slow one.

To take your first solitary bite
And move on your slow, solitary hunt.
Your bright, dark little eye,
Your eye of a dark disturbed night,
Under its slow lid, tiny baby tortoise,
So indomitable.

No one ever heard you complain.

You draw your head forward, slowly, from your little wimple
And set forward, slow-dragging, on your four-pinned toes,
Rowing slowly forward.
Whither away, small bird?

Rather like a baby working its limbs,
Except that you make slow, ageless progress
And a baby makes none.

The touch of sun excites you,
And the long ages, and the lingering chill
Make you pause to yawn,
Opening your impervious mouth,
Suddenly beak-shaped, and very wide, like some suddenly gaping
    pincers;
Soft red tongue, and hard thin gums,
Then close the wedge of your little mountain front,
Your face, baby tortoise.

Do you wonder at the world, as slowly you turn your head in its wimple
And look with laconic, black eyes?
Or is sleep coming over you again,
The non-life?

You are so hard to wake.

Are you able to wonder?
Or is it just your indomitable will and pride of the first life
Looking round
And slowly pitching itself against the inertia
Which had seemed invincible?

The vast inanimate,
And the fine brilliance of your so tiny eye,
Challenger.

Nay, tiny shell-bird,
What a huge vast inanimate it is, that you must row against,
What an incalculable inertia.

Challenger,
Little Ulysses, fore-runner,
No bigger than my thumb-nail,
Buon viaggio.

All animate creation on your shoulder,
Set forth, little Titan, under your battle-shield.

The ponderous, preponderate,
Inanimate universe;
And you are slowly moving, pioneer, you alone.

How vivid your travelling seems now, in the troubled sunshine,
Stoic, Ulyssean atom;
Suddenly hasty, reckless, on high toes.

Voiceless little bird,
Resting your head half out of your wimple
In the slow dignity of your eternal pause.
Alone, with no sense of being alone,
And hence six times more solitary;
Fulfilled of the slow passion of pitching through immemorial ages
Your little round house in the midst of chaos.

Over the garden earth,
Small bird,
Over the edge of all things.

Traveller,
With your tail tucked a little on one side
Like a gentleman in a long-skirted coat.

All life carried on your shoulder,
Invincible fore-runner.

Tortoise-Shell

The Cross, the Cross
Goes deeper in than we know,
Deeper into life;
Right into the marrow
And through the bone.

Along the back of the baby tortoise
The scales are locked in an arch like a bridge,
Scale-lapping, like a lobster's sections
Or a bee's.

Then crossways down his sides
Tiger-stripes and wasp-bands.

Five, and five again, and five again,
And round the edges twenty-five little ones,
The sections of the baby tortoise shell.

Four, and a keystone;
Four, and a keystone;
Four, and a keystone;
Then twenty-four, and a tiny little keystone.

It needed Pythagoras to see life placing her counters on the living back
Of the baby tortoise;
Life establishing the first eternal mathematical tablet,
Not in stone, like the Judean Lord, or bronze, but in life-clouded,
    life-rosy tortoise-shell.

The first little mathematical gentleman
Stepping, wee mite, in his loose trousers
Under all the eternal dome of mathematical law.

Fives, and tens,
Threes and fours and twelves,
All the volte face of decimals,
The whirligig of dozens and the pinnacle of seven.

Turn him on his back,
The kicking little beetle,
And there again, on his shell-tender, earth-touching belly,
The long cleavage of division, upright of the eternal cross
And on either side count five,
On each side, two above, on each side, two below
The dark bar horizontal.

The Cross!
It goes right through him, the sprottling insect,
Through his cross-wise cloven psyche,
Through his five-fold complex-nature.

So turn him over on his toes again;
Four pin-point toes, and a problematical thumb-piece,
Four rowing limbs, and one wedge-balancing head,
Four and one makes five, which is the clue to all mathematics.

The Lord wrote it all down on the little slate
Of the baby tortoise.
Outward and visible indication of the plan within,
The complex, manifold involvedness of an individual creature
Blotted out
On this small bird, this rudiment,
This little dome, this pediment
Of all creation,
This slow one.

Tortoise Family Connections

On he goes, the little one,
Bud of the universe,
Pediment of life.

Setting off somewhere, apparently.
Whither away, brisk egg?

His mother deposited him on the soil as if he were
    no more than droppings,
And now he scuffles tinily past her as if she were
    an old rusty tin.

A mere obstacle,
He veers round the slow great mound of her—
Tortoises always foresee obstacles.

It is no use my saying to him in an emotional voice:
"This is your Mother, she laid you when you were an egg."

He does not even trouble to answer: "Woman, what have I to
    do with thee?"
He wearily looks the other way,
And she even more wearily looks another way still,

Each with the utmost apathy,
Incognizant,
Unaware,
Nothing.

As for papa,
He snaps when I offer him his offspring,
Just as he snaps when I poke a bit of stick at him,
Because he is irascible this morning, an irascible tortoise
Being touched with love, and devoid of fatherliness.

Father and mother,
And three little brothers,
And all rambling aimless, like little perambulating
    pebbles scattered in the garden,
Not knowing each other from bits of earth or old tins.
Except that papa and mama are old acquaintances,
    of course,
But family feeling there is none, not even the beginnings.

Fatherless, motherless, brotherless, sisterless
Little tortoise.

Row on then, small pebble,
Over the clods of the autumn, wind-chilled sunshine,
Young gayety.

Does he look for a companion?

No, no, don't think it.
He doesn't know he is alone;
Isolation is his birthright,
This atom.

To row forward, and reach himself tall on spiny toes,
To travel, to burrow into a little loose earth, afraid of the night,
To crop a little substance,
To move, and to be quite sure that he is moving:
Basta!

To be a tortoise!
Think of it, in a garden of inert clods

A brisk, brindled little tortoise, all to himself—
Crœsus!

In a garden of pebbles and insects
To roam, and feel the slow heart beat
Tortoise-wise, the first bell sounding
From the warm blood, in the dark-creation morning.

Moving, and being himself,
Slow, and unquestioned,
And inordinately there, O stoic!
Wandering in the slow triumph of his own existence,
Ringing the soundless bell of his presence in chaos,
And biting the frail grass arrogantly,
Decidedly arrogantly.

Lui et Elle

She is large and matronly
And rather dirty,
A little sardonic-looking, as if domesticity had driven her to it.

Though what she does, except lay four eggs at random
    in the garden once a year
And put up with her husband,
I don't know.

She likes to eat.
She hurries up, striding reared on long uncanny legs,
When food is going.
Oh yes, she can make haste when she likes.

She snaps the soft bread from my hand in great mouthfuls,
Opening her rather pretty wedge of an iron, pristine face
Into an enormously wide-beaked mouth
Like sudden curved scissors,
And gulping at more than she can swallow, and working
    her thick, soft tongue,
And having the bread hanging over her chin.

O Mistress, Mistress,
Reptile mistress,
Your eye is very dark, very bright,
And it never softens
Although you watch.

She knows,
She knows well enough to come for food,
Yet she sees me not;
Her bright eye sees, but not me, not anything,
Sightful, sightless, seeing and visionless,
Reptile mistress.

Taking bread in her curved, gaping, toothless mouth,
She has no qualm when she catches my finger in her steel
overlapping gums,
But she hangs on, and my shout and my shrinking are nothing
    to her,
She does not even know she is nipping me with her curved beak.
Snake-like she draws at my finger, while I drag it in horror away.

Mistress, reptile mistress,
You are almost too large, I am almost frightened.

He is much smaller,
Dapper beside her,
And ridiculously small.

Her laconic eye has an earthy, materialistic look,
His, poor darling, is almost fiery.

His wimple, his blunt-prowed face,
His low forehead, his skinny neck, his long, scaled,
    striving legs,
So striving, striving,
Are all more delicate than she,
And he has a cruel scar on his shell.

Poor darling, biting at her feet,
Running beside her like a dog, biting her earthy, splay feet,
Nipping her ankles,

Which she drags apathetic away, though without retreating
    into her shell.

Agelessly silent,
And with a grim, reptile determination,
Cold, voiceless age-after-age behind him, serpents' long obstinacy
Of horizontal persistence.

Little old man
Scuffling beside her, bending down, catching his opportunity,
Parting his steel-trap face, so suddenly, and seizing her scaly ankle,
And hanging grimly on,
Letting go at last as she drags away,
And closing his steel-trap face.

His steel-trap, stoic, ageless, handsome face.
Alas, what a fool he looks in this scuffle.

And how he feels it!
The lonely rambler, the stoic, dignified stalker through chaos,
The immune, the animate,
Enveloped in isolation,
Forerunner.
Now look at him!

Alas, the spear is through the side of his isolation.
His adolescence saw him crucified into sex,
Doomed, in the long crucifixion of desire, to seek
    his consummation beyond himself.
Divided into passionate duality,
He, so finished and immune, now broken into
    desirous fragmentariness,
Doomed to make an intolerable fool of himself
In his effort toward completion again.

Poor little earthy house-inhabiting Osiris,
The mysterious bull tore him at adolescence into pieces,
And he must struggle after reconstruction, ignominiously.

And so behold him following the tail
Of that mud-hovel of his slowly-rambling spouse,
Like some unhappy bull at the tail of a cow,
But with more than bovine, grim, earth-dank persistence,

Suddenly seizing the ugly ankle as she stretches out to walk,
Roaming over the sods,
Or, if it happen to show, at her pointed, heavy tail
Beneath the low-dropping back-board of her shell.

Their two shells like doomed boats bumping,
Hers huge, his small;
Their splay feet rambling and rowing like paddles,
And stumbling mixed up in one another,
In the race of love—
Two tortoises,
She huge, he small.

She seems earthily apathetic,
And he has a reptile's awful persistence.

I heard a woman pitying her, pitying the Mère Tortue.
While I, I pity Monsieur.
"He pesters her and torments her," said the woman.
How much more is *he* pestered and tormented, say I.

What can he do?
He is dumb, he is visionless,
Conceptionless.
His black, sad-lidded eye sees but beholds not
As her earthen mound moves on,
But he catches the folds of vulnerable, leathery skin,
Nail-studded, that shake beneath her shell,
And drags at these with his beak,
Drags and drags and bites,
While she pulls herself free, and rows her dull mound along.

Tortoise Gallantry

Making his advances
He does not look at her, nor sniff at her,
No, not even sniff at her, his nose is blank.

Only he senses the vulnerable folds of skin
That work beneath her while she sprawls along
In her ungainly pace,

Her folds of skin that work and row
Beneath the earth-soiled hovel in which she moves.

And so he strains beneath her housey walls
And catches her trouser-legs in his beak
Suddenly, or her skinny limb,
And strange and grimly drags at her
Like a dog,
Only agelessly silent, with a reptile's awful persistency.

Grim, gruesome gallantry, to which he is doomed.
Dragging out of an eternity of silent isolation
And doomed to partiality, partial being,
Ache, and want of being,
Want,
Self-exposure, hard humiliation, need to add himself on to her.

Born to walk alone,
Forerunner,
Now suddenly distracted into this mazy sidetrack,
This awkward, harrowing pursuit,
This grim necessity from within.

Does she know
As she moves eternally slowly away?
Or is he driven against her with a bang, like a bird
   flying in the dark against a window,
All knowledgeless?

The awful concussion,
And the still more awful need to persist, to follow, follow, continue,
Driven, after æons of pristine, fore-god-like singleness and oneness,
At the end of some mysterious, red-hot iron,
Driven away from himself into her tracks,
Forced to crash against her.

Stiff, gallant, irascible, crook-legged reptile,
Little gentleman,
Sorry plight,
We ought to look the other way.

Save that, having come with you so far,
We will go on to the end.

Tortoise Shout

I thought he was dumb,
I said he was dumb,
Yet I've heard him cry.

First faint scream,
Out of life's unfathomable dawn,
Far off, so far, like a madness, under the horizon's dawning rim,
Far, far off, far scream.

Tortoise *in extremis*.

Why were we crucified into sex?
Why were we not left rounded off, and finished in ourselves,
As we began,
As he certainly began, so perfectly alone?

A far, was-it-audible scream,
Or did it sound on the plasm direct?
Worse than the cry of the new-born,
A scream,
A yell,
A shout,
A pæan,
A death-agony,
A birth-cry,
A submission,
All tiny, tiny, far away, reptile under the first dawn.

War-cry, triumph, acute-delight, death-scream reptilian,
Why was the veil torn?
The silken shriek of the soul's torn membrane?
The male soul's membrane
Torn with a shriek half music, half horror.

Crucifixion.
Male tortoise, cleaving behind the hovel-wall of that dense female,
Mounted and tense, spread-eagle, out-reaching out of the shell
In tortoise-nakedness,
Long neck, and long vulnerable limbs extruded, spread-eagle
   over her house-roof,

And the deep, secret, all-penetrating tail curved beneath her walls,
Reaching and gripping tense, more reaching anguish
    in uttermost tension
Till suddenly, in the spasm of coition, tupping like a
    jerking leap, and oh!
Opening its clenched face from his outstretched neck
And giving that fragile yell, that scream,
Super-audible,
From his pink, cleft, old-man's mouth,
Giving up the ghost,
Or screaming in Pentecost, receiving the ghost.

His scream, and his moment's subsidence,
The moment of eternal silence,
Yet unreleased, and after the moment, the sudden, startling
    jerk of coition, and at once
The inexpressible faint yell—
And so on, till the last plasm of my body was melted back
To the primeval rudiments of life, and the secret.

So he tups, and screams
Time after time that frail, torn scream
After each jerk, the longish interval,
The tortoise eternity,
Agelong, reptilian persistence,
Heart-throb, slow heart-throb, persistent for the next spasm.

I remember, when I was a boy,
I heard the scream of a frog, which was caught with his foot
    in the mouth of an up-starting snake;
I remember when I first heard bull-frogs break into sound
    in the spring;
I remember hearing a wild goose out of the throat of night
Cry loudly, beyond the lake of waters;
I remember the first time, out of a bush in the darkness,
    a nightingale's piercing cries and gurgles startled the depths of my soul;
I remember the scream of a rabbit as I went through a wood at midnight;
I remember the heifer in her heat, blorting and blorting through the hours,
    persistent and irrepressible;

I remember my first terror of hearing the howl of weird,
    amorous cats;
I remember the scream of a terrified, injured horse,
    the sheet-lightning
And running away from the sound of a woman in labor,
    something like an owl whooing,
And listening inwardly to the first bleat of a lamb,
The first wail of an infant,
And my mother singing to herself,
And the first tenor singing of the passionate throat
    of a young collier, who has long since drunk himself to death,
The first elements of foreign speech
On wild dark lips.

And more than all these,
And less than all these,
This last,
Strange, faint coition yell
Of the male tortoise at extremity,
Tiny from under the very edge of the farthest far-off horizon of life.

The cross,
The wheel on which our silence first is broken,
Sex, which breaks up our integrity, our single inviolability,
    our deep silence
Tearing a cry from us.

Sex, which breaks us into voice, sets us calling
    across the deeps, calling, calling for the complement,
Singing, and calling, and singing again, being answered,
    having found.

Torn, to become whole again, after long seeking for what is lost,
The same cry from the tortoise as from Christ, the Osiris-cry
    of abandonment,
That which is whole, torn asunder,
That which is in part, finding its whole again throughout the universe.

Snake

A snake came to my water-trough
On a hot, hot day, and I in pyjamas for the heat,
To drink there.

In the deep, strange-scented shade of the great dark carob tree
I came down the steps with my pitcher
And must wait, must stand and wait, for there he was at the trough
    before me.

He reached down from a fissure in the earth-wall in the gloom
And trailed his yellow-brown slackness soft-bellied down, over the
    edge of the stone trough
And rested his throat upon the stone bottom,
And where the water had dripped from the tap, in a small clearness,
He sipped with his straight mouth,
Softly drank through his straight gums, into his slack long body,
Silently.

Someone was before me at my water-trough,
And I, like a second-comer, waiting.

He lifted his head from his drinking, as cattle do,
And looked at me vaguely, as drinking cattle do,
And flickered his two-forked tongue from his lips, and mused a moment,
And stooped and drank a little more,
Being earth-brown, earth-golden from the burning bowels of the earth
On the day of Sicilian July, with Etna smoking.

The voice of my education said to me
He must be killed,
For in Sicily the black, black snakes are innocent, the gold are
    venomous.

And voices in me said, If you were a man
You would take a stick and break him now, and finish him off.

But must I confess how I liked him,
How glad I was he had come like a guest in quiet, to drink at my
    water-trough
And depart peaceful, pacified, and thankless,
Into the burning bowels of this earth?

Was it cowardice, that I dared not kill him?
Was it perversity, that I longed to talk to him?
Was it humility, to feel honoured?
I felt so honoured.

And yet those voices:
If you were not afraid you would kill him.

And truly I was afraid, I was most afraid,
But even so, honoured still more
That he should seek my hospitality
From out the dark door of the secret earth.

He drank enough
And lifted his head, dreamily, as one who has drunken,
And flickered his tongue like a forked night on the air, so black,
Seeming to lick his lips,
And looked around like a god, unseeing into the air,
And slowly turned his head,
And slowly, very slowly, as if thrice adream,
Proceeded to draw his slow length curving round
And climb again the broken bank of my wall-face.

And as he put his head into that dreadful hole,
And as he slowly drew up, snake-easing his shoulders, and entered
    further,
A sort of horror, a sort of protest against his withdrawing into that horrid
    black hole,
Deliberately going into the blackness, and slowly drawing himself after,
Overcame me now his back was turned.

I looked round, I put down my pitcher,
I picked up a clumsy log
And threw it at the water-trough with a clatter.

I think it did not hit him,
But suddenly that part of him that was left behind convulsed in
undignified haste,
Writhed like lightning, and was gone
Into the black hole, the earth-lipped fissure in the wall-front,
At which, in the intense still noon, I stared with fascination.

And immediately I regretted it.
I thought how paltry, how vulgar, what a mean act!
I despised myself and the voices of my accursed human education.

And I thought of the albatross,
And I wished he would come back, my snake.

For he seemed to me again like a king,
Like a king in exile, uncrowned in the underworld,
Now due to be crowned again.

And so, I missed my chance with one of the lords
Of life.
And I have something to expiate:
A pettiness.

Fish

Fish, oh Fish,
So little matters!

Whether the waters rise and cover the earth
Or whether the waters wilt in the hollow places,
All one to you.

Aqueous, subaqueous,
Submerged
And wave-thrilled.

As the waters roll
Roll you.
The waters wash,
You wash in oneness
And never emerge.

Never know,
Never grasp.

Your life a sluice of sensation along your sides,
A flush at the flails of your fins, down the whorl of your tail,
And water wetly on fire in the grates of your gills;
Fixed water-eyes.

Even snakes lie together.

But oh, fish, that rock in water,
You lie only with the waters;
One touch.

Quelle joie de vivre
Dans l'eau!
Slowly to gape through the waters,
Alone with the element;
To sink, and rise, and go to sleep with the waters;
To speak endless inaudible wavelets into the wave;
To breathe from the flood at the gills,
Fish blood slowly running next to the flood, extracting fish-fire;
To have the element under one, like a lover;
And to spring away with a curveting click in the air,
Provocative.
Dropping back with a slap on the face of the flood
And merging oneself!

To be a fish!

So utterly without misgiving
To be a fish
In the waters.

Loveless, and so lively!
Born before God was love,
Or life knew loving.
Beautifully beforehand with it all.

Admitted, they swarm in companies,
Fishes.
They drive in shoals.
But soundless, and out of contact.
They exchange no word, no spasm, not even anger.
Not one touch.
Many suspended together, forever apart,
Each one alone with the waters, upon one wave with the rest.
A magnetism in the water between them only.

I saw a water-serpent swim across the Anapo,
And I said to my heart, Look, look at him!

With his head up, steering like a bird!
He's a rare one, but he belongs. . . .

But sitting in a boat on the Zeller lake
And watching the fishes in the breathing waters
Lift and swim and go their way—
I said to my heart, Who are these?
And my heart couldn't own them. . . .

A slim young pike, with smart fins
And grey-striped suit, a young cub of a pike
Slouching along away below, half out of sight,
Like a lout on an obscure pavement. . . .

Aha, there's somebody in the know!

But watching closer
That motionless deadly motion,
That unnatural barrel body, that long ghoul nose . . .
I left off hailing him.

I had made a mistake, I didn't know him,
This grey, monotonous soul in the water,
This intense individual in shadow,
Fish alive.

I didn't know his God,
I didn't know his God.

Which is perhaps the last admission that life has to wring out of us.

I saw, dimly,
Once a big pike rush,
And small fish fly like splinters.
And I said to my heart, There are limits
To you, my heart;
And to the one God.
Fish are beyond me.

Other Gods
Beyond my range . . . gods beyond my God. . . .

They are beyond me, are fishes.
I stand at the pale of my being
And look beyond, and see
Fish, in the outerwards,
As one stands on a bank and looks in.

I have waited with a long rod
And suddenly pulled a gold-and-greenish, lucent fish from below,
And had him fly like a halo round my head,
Lunging in the air on the line.

Unhooked his gorping, water-horny mouth,
And seen his horror-tilted eye,
His red-gold, water-precious, mirror-flat bright eye;
And felt him beat in my hand, with his mucous, leaping lifethrob.

And my heart accused itself,
Thinking: *I am not the measure of creation.*
This is beyond me, this fish.
His God stands outside my God.

And the gold-and-green pure lacquer-mucous comes off in my hand,
And the red-gold mirror-eye stares and dies,
And the water-suave contour dims.

But not before I have had to know
He was born in front of my sunrise,
Before my day.
He outstarts me.
And I, a many-fingered horror of daylight to him,
Have made him die.

Fishes,
With their gold-red eyes, and green-pure gleam, and under-gold,
And their pre-world loneliness,
And more-than-lovelessness,
And white flesh;
They move in other circles.

Outsiders.
Water wayfarers.

Things of one element.
Aqueous,
Each by itself.

Cats, and the Neapolitans,
Sulphur sun-beasts,
Thirst for fish as for more-than-water;
Water alive
To quench their over-sulphureous lusts.

But I, I only wonder
And don't know.
I don't know fishes.

In the beginning
Jesus was called The Fish . . .
And in the end.

Bat

At evening, sitting on this terrace,
When the sun from the west, beyond Pisa, beyond the mountains of
    Carrara
Departs, and the world is taken by surprise. . . .

When the tired flower of Florence is in gloom beneath the glowing
Brown hills surrounding. . . .

When under the arches of the Ponte Vecchio
A green light enters against stream, flush from the west,
Against the current of obscure Arno. . . .

Look up, and you see things flying
Between the day and the night;
Swallows with spools of dark thread sewing the shadows together.

A circle swoop, and a quick parabola under the bridge arches
Where light pushes through;
A sudden turning upon itself of a thing in the air.
A dip to the water.

And you think:
"The swallows are flying so late!"

Swallows?

Dark air-life looping
Yet missing the pure loop . . .
A twitch, a twitter, an elastic shudder in flight,
And serrated wings against the sky,
Like a glove, a black glove thrown up at the light,
And falling back.

Never swallows!
Bats!
The swallows are gone.

At a wavering instant the swallows gave way to bats
By the Ponte Vecchio . . .
Changing guard.

Bats, and an uneasy creeping in one's scalp
As the bats swoop overhead!
Flying madly.

Pipistrello!
Black piper on an infinitesimal pipe.
Little lumps that fly in air and have voices indefinite,
    wildly vindictive,
Wings like bits of umbrella.

Bats!

Creatures that hang themselves up like an old rag, to sleep;
And disgustingly upside down.

Hanging upside down like rows of disgusting old rags
And grinning in their sleep.
Bats!

Not for me!

The Mosquito

When did you start your tricks,
　Monsieur?

What do you stand on such high legs for?
Why this length of shredded shank,
You exaltation?

Is it so that you shall lift your centre of gravity upwards
And weigh no more than air as you alight upon me,
Stand upon me weightless, you phantom?

I heard a woman call you the Winged Victory
In sluggish Venice.
You turn your head toward your tail, and smile.

How can you put so much devilry
In that translucent phantom shred
Of a frail corpus?

Queer, with your thin wings and your streaming legs
How you sail like a heron, or a dull clot of air,
A nothingness.

Yet what an aura surrounds you;
Your evil little aura, prowling, and casting a numbness on my mind.

That is your trick, your bit of filthy magic:
Invisibility, and the anæsthetic power
To deaden my attention in your direction.
But I know your game now, streaky sorcerer.

Queer, how you stalk and prowl the air
In circles and evasions, enveloping me,
Ghoul on wings,
Winged Victory.

Settle, and stand on long thin shanks,
Eyeing me sideways, and cunningly conscious that I am aware,
You speck.

I hate the way you lurch off sideways into air,
Having read my thoughts against you.

Come then, let us play at unawares,
And see who wins in this sly game of bluff,
Man or mosquito.

You don't know that I exist, and I don't know that you exist.
Now then!

It is your trump,
It is your hateful little trump,
You pointed fiend,
Which shakes my sudden blood to hatred of you;
It is your small, high, hateful bugle in my ear.

Why do you do it?
Surely it is bad policy.

They say you can't help it.

If that is so, then I believe a little in Providence protecting the innocent.
But it sounds so amazingly like a slogan,
A yell of triumph as you snatch my scalp.

Blood, red blood,
Super-magical,
Forbidden liquor.

I behold you stand
For a second enspasmed in oblivion,
Obscenely ecstasied,
Sucking live blood,
My blood.

Such silence, such suspended transport,
Such gorging,
Such obscenity of trespass.

You stagger
As well you may;
Only your accursed hairy frailty,

Your own imponderable weightlessness,
Saves you, wafts you away on the very draught my anger makes in its
 snatching.

Away with a pæan of derision,
You winged blood-drop.

Can I not overtake you?
Are you one too many for me,
Winged Victory?
Am I not mosquito enough to out-mosquito you?

Queer, what a big stain my blood makes
Beside the infinitesimal faint smear of you!
Queer, what a dim dark smudge you have disappeared into!

Humming-Bird

I can imagine, in some otherworld
Primeval-dumb, far back
In that most awful stillness, that only gasped and hummed,
Humming-birds raced down the avenue.

Before anything had a soul,
While life was a heave of matter, half inanimate,
This little bit chipped off in brilliance
And went whizzing through the slow, vast, succulent stems.

I believe there were no flowers then
In the world where the humming-bird flashed ahead of creation;
I believe he pierced the slow vegetable veins with his long beak.

Probably he was big,
As mosses, and little lizards, they say were once big;
Probably he was a jabbing, terrifying monster.

We look at him through the wrong end of the telescope of Time,
Luckily for us.

Pomegranate

You tell me I am wrong.
Who are you, who is anybody, to tell me I am wrong?
I am not wrong.

In Syracuse, rock left bare by the viciousness of Greek women,
No doubt you have forgotten the pomegranate trees in flower,
Oh, so red, and such a lot of them.

Whereas at Venice,
Abhorrent, green, grey-bearded,
Whose Doges are old and had ancient eyes,
In the dense foliage of the inner garden
Pomegranates like bright green stones,
And barbed, barbed with a crown,
Oh, horrible crown, of spiked green metal,
Actually were growing.

Now, in Tuscany
Pomegranates to warm your hands at,
Braziers,
And crowns,
Kingly, generous, tilting crowns,
Over the left eyebrow.

And, if you dare, the fissure!

Do you mean to tell me you will see no fissure?
You prefer to look on the plain side?
For all that, the setting suns are open,
The last day fissured open with to-morrow,
Rosy, tender, glittering within there.

Do you mean to tell me there should be no fissure?
No glittering compact drops of dawn?
Do you mean it is wrong, the gold-filmed skin, integument,
    shown ruptured?

For my part, I prefer my heart to be broken.
It is so lovely, dawn-kaleidoscopic, within the crack.

Medlars and Sorb-Apples

I love you, rotten.
Delicious rottenness!

I love to suck you out from your skins,
So brown and soft and coming suave,
So morbid, as the Italians say.

What a rare, powerful, reminiscent flavour
Comes out of your falling through the stages of decay,
Stream within stream!

Something of the same flavour as Syracusan muscat wine
Or vulgar Marsala.

Though even the word Marsala will smack of preciosity
Now in the pussy-foot West.

What is it?
What is it in the grape turning raisin,
In the medlar, in the sorb-apple,
Wineskins of brown morbidity,
Autumnal excrementa,
What is that reminds us of white gods?

Gods, nude as blanched nut-kernels,
Strangely, half-sinisterly flesh-fragrant
As if with sweat,
And drenched with mystery?
Sorb-apples, medlars with dead crowns.

I say, wonderful are the hellish experiences,
Orphic, delicate
Dionysos of the Underworld.

A kiss, and a vivid spasm of farewell, a moment's orgasm of rupture,
Then along the damp road alone, till the next turning.
And there, a new partner, a new parting, a new unfusing into twain,
A new gasp of further isolation,
A new intoxication of loneliness, among decaying frost-cold leaves.

Going down the strange lanes of hell, more and more intensely alone,
The fibres of the heart parting one after the other,
And yet the soul continuing, naked-footed, ever more vividly embodied,
Like a flame blown whiter and whiter
In a deeper and deeper darkness,
Ever more exquisite, distilled in separation.

So, in the strange retorts of medlars and sorb-apples
The distilled essence of hell.
The exquisite fragrance of leave-taking. *Jamque vale!*
Orpheus, and the winding, leaf-clogged, silent lanes of Hell.

Each soul departing with its own isolation,
Strangest of all strange companions,
And best.

Medlars, sorb-apples,
More than sweet,
Flux of autumn,
Sucked out of your empty bladders
And sipped down, perhaps, with a sip of Marsala
So that the rambling, sky-dropped grape can add its music to yours,
Orphic farewell, and farewell, and farewell,
And the *ego sum* of Dionysos,
The *sono io* of perfect drunkenness,
Intoxication of final loneliness.

DOVER · THRIFT · EDITIONS

All books complete and unabridged. All 5⁵⁄₁₆ x 8¹⁄₄, paperbound.
Just $1.00—$2.00 in U.S.A.

A selection of the more than 200 titles in the series.